Ultra Tasty Sirtfood Diet Recipes – 2 Books in 1

Activate Your Skinny Gene, Lose Weight and Burn Fat with These Incredible Sirt Recipes

By

Lara Middleton

Sirt Diet Recipes for Breakfast

by

Lara Middleton

Additionally, the information in the following pages is intended only for informational purposes and should thus be thought of as universal. As befitting its nature, it is presented without assurance regarding its prolonged validity or interim quality. Trademarks that are mentioned are done without written consent and can in no way be considered an endorsement from the trademark holder.

Table of Contents

Matcha Green Juice

Preparation time: 10 minutes

Cooking time: 0 minutes

Servings: 2

Ingredients:

- 5 ounces fresh kale

- 2 ounces fresh arugula

- ¼ cup fresh parsley

- 4 celery stalks

- 1 green apple, cored and chopped

- 1 (1-inch) piece fresh ginger, peeled

- 1 lemon, peeled

- ½ teaspoon matcha green tea

Directions:

- Add all ingredients into a juicer and extract the juice according to the manufacturer's method.

- Pour into 2 glasses and serve immediately.

Nutrition:

- Calories: 113

- Fat: 0.6 g

- Carbohydrates: 26.71 g

- Protein: 3.8 g

Celery Juice

Preparation time: 10 minutes

Cooking time: 0 minutes

Servings: 2

Ingredients:

- 8 celery stalks with leaves

- 2 tablespoons fresh ginger, peeled

- 1 lemon, peeled

- ½ cup filtered water

- Pinch of salt

Directions:

- Place all the ingredients in a blender and pulse until well combined.

- Through a fine mesh strainer, strain the juice and transfer into 2 glasses.

- Serve immediately.

Nutrition:

- Calories: 32

- Fat: 0.5 g

- Carbohydrates: 6.5 g

- Protein: 1 g

Kale & Orange Juice

Preparation time: 10 minutes

Cooking time: 0 minutes

Servings: 2

Ingredients:

- 5 large oranges, peeled and sectioned

- 2 bunches fresh kale

Directions:

- Add all ingredients into a juicer and extract the juice according to the manufacturer's method.

- Pour into 2 glasses and serve immediately.

16

Nutrition:

- Calories: 315

- Fat: 0.6 g

- Carbohydrates: 75.1 g

- Protein: 10.3 g

Apple & Cucumber Juice

Preparation time: 10 minutes

Cooking time: 0 minutes

Servings: 2

Ingredients:

- 3 large apples, cored and sliced

- 2 large cucumbers, sliced

- 4 celery stalks

- 1 (1-inch) piece fresh ginger, peeled

- 1 lemon, peeled

Directions:

- Add all ingredients into a juicer and extract the juice according to the manufacturer's method.

- Pour into 2 glasses and serve immediately.

Nutrition:

- Calories: 230

- Fat: 1.1 g

- Carbohydrates: 59.5 g

- Protein: 3.3 g

Lemony Green Juice

Preparation time: 10 minutes

Cooking time: 0 minutes

Servings: 2

Ingredients:

- 2 large green apples, cored and sliced

- 4 cups fresh kale leaves

- 4 tablespoons fresh parsley leaves

- 1 tablespoon fresh ginger, peeled

- 1 lemon, peeled

- ½ cup filtered water

- Pinch of salt

Directions:

- Place all the ingredients in a blender and pulse until well combined.

- Through a fine mesh strainer, strain the juice and transfer into 2 glasses.

- Serve immediately.

Nutrition:

- Calories: 196

- Fat: 0.6 g

- Carbohydrates: 47.9 g

- Protein: 5.2 g

Kale Scramble

Preparation time: 10 minutes

Cooking time: 6 minutes

Servings: 2

Ingredients:

- 4 eggs

- 1/8 teaspoon ground turmeric

- Salt and ground black pepper, to taste

- 1 tablespoon water

23

- 2 teaspoons olive oil

- 1 cup fresh kale, tough ribs removed and chopped

Directions:

- In a bowl, add the eggs, turmeric, salt, black pepper, and water and with a whisk, beat until foamy.

- In a wok, heat the oil over medium heat.

- Add the egg mixture and stir to combine.

- Immediately, reduce the heat to medium-low and cook for about 1–2 minutes, stirring frequently.

- Stir in the kale and cook for about 3–4 minutes, stirring frequently.

- Remove from the heat and serve immediately.

Nutrition:

- Calories: 183

- Fat: 13.4 g

- Carbohydrates: 4.3 g

- Protein: 12.1 g

Buckwheat Porridge

Preparation time: 10 minutes

Cooking time: 15 minutes

Servings: 2

Ingredients:

- 1 cup buckwheat, rinsed

- 1 cup unsweetened almond milk

- 1 cup water

- ½ teaspoon ground cinnamon

- ½ teaspoon vanilla extract

- 1–2 tablespoons raw honey

- ¼ cup fresh blueberries

Directions:

- In a pan, add all the ingredients (except honey and blueberries) over medium-high heat and bring to a boil.

- Now, reduce the heat to low and simmer, covered for about 10 minutes.

- Stir in the honey and remove from the heat.

- Set aside, covered, for about 5 minutes.

- With a fork, fluff the mixture, and transfer into serving bowls.

- Top with blueberries and serve.

Nutrition:

- Calories: 358

- Fat: 4.7 g

- Carbohydrates: 3.7 g

- Protein: 12 g

Blueberry Muffins

Preparation time: 15 minutes

Cooking time: 20 minutes

Servings: 8

Ingredients

- 1 cup buckwheat flour

- ¼ cup arrowroot starch

- 1½ teaspoons baking powder

- ¼ teaspoon sea salt

- 2 eggs

- ½ cup unsweetened almond milk

- 2–3 tablespoons maple syrup

- 2 tablespoons coconut oil, melted

- 1 cup fresh blueberries

Directions:

- Preheat your oven to 350°F and line 8 cups of a muffin tin.

- In a bowl, place the buckwheat flour, arrowroot starch, baking powder, and salt, and mix well.

- In a separate bowl, place the eggs, almond milk, maple syrup, and coconut oil, and beat until well combined.

- Now, place the flour mixture and mix until just combined.

- Gently, fold in the blueberries.

- Transfer the mixture into prepared muffin cups evenly.

- Bake for about 25 minutes or until a toothpick inserted in the center comes out clean.

- Remove the muffin tin from oven and place onto a wire rack to cool for about 10 minutes.

- Carefully invert the muffins onto the wire rack to cool completely before serving.

Nutrition:

- Calories: 136

- Fat: 5.3 g

- Carbohydrates: 20.7 g

- Protein: 3.5 g

Chocolate Waffles

Preparation time: 15 minutes

Cooking time: 24 minutes

Servings: 8

Ingredients

- 2 cups unsweetened almond milk

- 1 tablespoon fresh lemon juice

- 1 cup buckwheat flour

- ½ cup cacao powder

- ¼ cup flaxseed meal

- 1 teaspoon baking soda

- 1 teaspoon baking powder

- ¼ teaspoons kosher salt

- 2 large eggs

- ½ cup coconut oil, melted

- ¼ cup dark brown sugar

- 2 teaspoons vanilla extract

- 2 ounces unsweetened dark chocolate, chopped roughly

Directions:

- In a bowl, add the almond milk and lemon juice and mix well.

- Set aside for about 10 minutes.

- In a bowl, place buckwheat flour, cacao powder, flaxseed meal, baking soda, baking powder, and salt, and mix well.

- In the bowl of almond milk mixture, place the eggs, coconut oil, brown sugar, and vanilla extract, and beat until smooth.

- Now, place the flour mixture and beat until smooth.

- Gently, fold in the chocolate pieces.

- Preheat the waffle iron and then grease it.

- Place the desired amount of the mixture into the preheated waffle iron and cook for about 3 minutes, or until golden-brown.

- Repeat with the remaining mixture.

Nutrition:

- Calories: 295

- Fat: 22.1 g

- Carbohydrates: 1.5 g

- Protein: 6.3 g

Moroccan Spiced Eggs

Preparation time: 1 hour

Cooking time: 50 minutes

Servings: 2

Ingredients:

- 1 tsp. olive oil

- 1 shallot, stripped and finely hacked

- 1 red (chime) pepper, deseeded and finely hacked

- 1 garlic clove, stripped and finely hacked

- 1 courgette (zucchini), stripped and finely hacked

- 1 tbsp. tomato purees (glue)

- ½ tsp. gentle stew powder

- ¼ tsp. ground cinnamon

- ¼ tsp. ground cumin

- ½ tsp. salt

- 1 × 400g (14oz) can hack tomatoes

- 1 x 400g (14oz) may chickpeas in water

- A little bunch of level leaf parsley (10g (1/3oz)), cleaved

- Four medium eggs at room temperature

Directions:

- Heat the oil in a pan; include the shallot and red (ringer) pepper and fry delicately for 5 minutes. At that point include the garlic and courgette (zucchini) and cook for one more moment or two. Include the tomato puree (glue), flavour and salt and mix through.

- Add the cleaved tomatoes and chickpeas (dousing alcohol and all) and increment the warmth to medium. With the top of the dish, stew the sauce for 30 minutes – ensure it is delicately rising all through and permit it to lessen in volume by around 33%.

- Remove from the warmth and mix in the cleaved parsley.

- Preheat the grill to 200C/180C fan/350F.

- When you are prepared to cook the eggs, bring the tomato sauce up to a delicate stew and move to a little broiler confirmation dish.

- Crack the eggs on the dish and lower them delicately into the stew. Spread with thwart and prepare in the grill for 10-15 minutes. Serve the blend in unique dishes with the eggs coasting on the top.

Nutrition:

- Calories: 116 kcal

- Protein: 6.97 g

- Fat: 5.22 g

- Carbohydrates: 13.14 g

Chilaquiles with Gochujang

Preparation time: 30 minutes

Cooking time: 20 minutes

Servings: 2

Ingredients:

- 1 dried ancho Chile

- 2 cups of water

- 1 cup squashed tomatoes

- 2 cloves of garlic

41

- 1 teaspoon genuine salt

- 1/2 tablespoons Gochujang

- 5 to 6 cups tortilla chips

- 3 enormous eggs

- 1 tablespoon olive oil

Directions:

- Get the water to heat a pot. I cheated marginally and heated the water in an electric pot and emptied it into the pan.

- Add the anchor Chile to the bubbled water and drench for 15 minutes to give it an opportunity to stout up.

- When completed, use tongs or a spoon to extricate Chili. Make sure to spare the water for the sauce.

- Mix the doused Chili, 1 cup of saved high temp water, squashed tomatoes, garlic, salt and gochujang.

- Empty sauce into a large dish and heat 4 to 5 minutes. Heat and include the tortilla chips.

- Mix the chips to cover with the sauce. In a different skillet, shower a teaspoon of oil and fry an egg on top, until the whites have settled.

- Plate the egg and cook the remainder of the eggs. Sear the eggs while you heat the red sauce.

- Top the chips with the seared eggs, cotija, hacked cilantro, jalapeños, onions and avocado. Serve right away.

Nutrition:

- Calories: 484 kcal

- Protein: 14.55 g

- Fat: 18.62 g

- Carbohydrates: 64.04 g

Twice Baked Breakfast Potatoes

Preparation time: 1 hour 10 minutes

Cooking time: 1 hour

Servings: 2

Ingredients:

- 2 medium reddish brown potatoes, cleaned and pricked with a fork everywhere

- 2 tablespoons unsalted spread

- 3 tablespoons overwhelming cream

- 4 rashers cooked bacon

44

- 4 huge eggs

- ½ cup destroyed cheddar

- Daintily cut chives

- Salt and pepper to taste

Directions:

- Preheat grill to 400°F.

- Spot potatoes straightforwardly on stove rack in the focal point of the grill and prepare for 30 to 45 min.

- Evacuate and permit potatoes to cool for around 15 minutes.

- Cut every potato down the middle longwise and burrow every half out, scooping the potato substance into a blending bowl.

- Gather margarine and cream to the potato and pound into a single unit until smooth — season with salt and pepper and mix.

- Spread a portion of the potato blend into the base of each emptied potato skin and sprinkle with one tablespoon cheddar (you may make them remain pounded potato left to snack on).

- Add bacon to every half and top with a raw egg.

- Spot potatoes onto a heating sheet and come back to the appliance.

- Lower broiler temperature to 375°F and heat potatoes until egg whites simply set and yolks are as yet runny.

- Top every potato with a sprinkle of the rest of the cheddar, season with salt and pepper and finish with cut chives.

Nutrition:

- Calories: 647 kcal

- Protein: 30.46 g

- Fat: 55.79 g

- Carbohydrates: 7.45 g

Sirt Muesli

Preparation time: 30 minutes

Cooking time: 0 minutes

Servings: 2

Ingredients:

- 20g buckwheat drops

- 10g buckwheat puffs

- 15g coconut drops or dried up coconut

48

- 40g Medjool dates, hollowed and slashed

- 15g pecans, slashed

- 10g cocoa nibs

- 100g strawberries, hulled and slashed

- 100g plain Greek yoghurt (or vegetarian elective, for example, soya or coconut yoghurt)

Directions:

- Blend all the ingredients then put strawberries and yoghurt.

- Serve immediately.

Nutrition:

- Calories: 334 kcal

- Protein: 4.39 g

- Fat: 22.58 g

- Carbohydrates: 34.35 g

Spiced Scramble

Preparation time: 5 minutes

Cooking time: 5 minutes

Servings: 1

Ingredients:

- 25g (1oz) kale, finely chopped

- 2 eggs

- 1 spring onion (scallion) finely chopped

- 1 teaspoon turmeric

- 1 tablespoon olive oil

- Sea salt

- Freshly ground black pepper

Directions:

- Crack the eggs into a bowl. Add the turmeric and whisk them and season with salt and pepper.

- Heat the oil in a frying pan, add the kale and spring onions (scallions) and cook until it has wilted.

- Pour in the beaten eggs and stir until eggs have scrambled together with the kale.

Nutrition:

- Calories: 218

- Total Fat: 15.3 g

- Cholesterol: 386.9 mg

- Sodium: 656.2 mg

- Potassium: 243.0 mg

- Carbohydrates: 2.8 g

- Protein: 17.4 g

Cheesy Baked Eggs

Preparation time: 5 minutes

Cooking time: 15 minutes

Servings: 4

Ingredients:

- 4 large eggs

- 75g (3oz) cheese, grated

- 25g (1oz) fresh rocket (arugula) leaves, finely chopped

- 1 tablespoon parsley

- ½ teaspoon ground turmeric

- 1 tablespoon olive oil

Directions:

- Grease each ramekin dish with a little olive oil. Divide the rocket (arugula) between the ramekin dishes then break an egg into each one.

- Sprinkle a little parsley and turmeric on top then sprinkle on the cheese.

- Place the ramekins in a preheated oven at 220C/425F for 15 minutes, until the eggs are set and the cheese is bubbling.

Nutrition:

- Calories: 67

- Total Fat: 4 g

- Cholesterol: 12 mg

- Sodium: 265 mg

- Potassium: 84 mg

- Total Carbohydrates: 0.2 g

- Protein: 8 g

Chilled Strawberry and Walnut Porridge

Preparation time: 10 minutes

Cooking time: 12 hours

Servings: 1

Ingredients:

- 100g (3½ oz) strawberries

- 50g (2oz) rolled oats

- 4 walnut halves, chopped

- 1 teaspoon chia seeds

- 200mls (7fl oz) unsweetened soya milk

- 100ml (3½ oz) water

Directions:

- Place the strawberries, oats, soya milk and water into a blender and process until smooth.

- Stir in the chia seeds and mix well.

- Chill in the fridge overnight and serve in the morning with a sprinkling of chopped walnuts. It's simple and delicious.

Nutrition:

- Calories: 242

- Total Fat: 6 g

- Cholesterol: 1.3 mg

- Sodium: 37 mg

- Potassium: 207 mg

- Carbohydrates: 45 g

- Protein: 6 g

Strawberry & Nut Granola

Preparation time: 10 minutes

Cooking time: 50 minutes

Servings: 12

Ingredients:

- 200g (7oz) oats

- 250g (9oz) buckwheat flakes

- 100g (3½ oz) walnuts, chopped

- 100g (3½ oz) almonds, chopped

- 100g (3½ oz) dried strawberries

- 1½ teaspoons ground ginger

- 1½ teaspoons ground cinnamon

- 120mls (4fl oz) olive oil

- 2 tablespoon honey

Directions:

- Combine the oats, buckwheat flakes, nuts, ginger and cinnamon.

- In a saucepan, warm the oil and honey. Stir until the honey has melted.

- Pour the warm oil into the dry ingredients and mix well.

- Spread the mixture out on a large baking tray (or two) and bake in the oven at 150C (300F) for around 50 minutes until the granola is golden.

- Allow it to cool. Add in the dried berries.

Nutrition:

- Calories: 220

- Fat: 3 g

- Carbohydrates: 44 g

- Protein: 6 g

-

Strawberry Buckwheat Pancakes

Preparation time: 10 minutes

Cooking time: 20 minutes

Servings: 4

Ingredients:

- 100g (3½oz) strawberries, chopped

- 100g (3½ oz) buckwheat flour

- 1 egg

- 250mls (8fl oz) milk

63

- 1 teaspoon olive oil

- 1 teaspoon olive oil for frying

- Freshly squeezed juice of 1 orange

Directions:

- Pour the milk into a bowl and mix in the egg and a teaspoon of olive oil.

- Sift in the flour to the liquid mixture until smooth and creamy.

- Allow it to rest for 15 minutes. Heat a little oil in a pan and pour in a quarter of the mixture (or to the size you prefer.)

- Sprinkle in a quarter of the strawberries into the batter.

- Cook for around 2 minutes on each side.

- Serve hot with a drizzle of orange juice.

- You could try experimenting with other berries such as blueberries and blackberries.

Nutrition:

- Calories: 76

- Fat: 3 g

- Cholesterol: 26 mg

- Sodium: 184 mg

- Potassium: 17 mg

- Carbohydrates: 4 g

- Protein: 2 g

Poached Eggs & Rocket (Arugula)

Preparation time: 3 minutes

Cooking time: 5 minutes

Servings: 2

Ingredients:

- 2 eggs

- 25g (1oz) fresh rocket (arugula)

- 1 teaspoon olive oil

- Sea salt

- Freshly ground black pepper

Directions:

- Scatter the rocket (arugula) leaves onto a plate and drizzle the olive oil over them.

- Bring a shallow pan of water to the boil, add in the eggs and cook until the whites become firm.

- Serve the eggs on top of the rocket and season with salt and pepper.

Nutrition:

- Calories: 166

- Total Fat: 10 g

- Total Carbohydrates: 7 g

- Protein: 12 g

Chocolate Berry Blend

Preparation time: 5 minutes

Cooking time: 5 minutes

Servings: 1

Ingredients:

- 50g (2oz) blueberries

- 50g (2oz) strawberries

- 1 tablespoon 100% cocoa powder or cacao nibs

- 200mls (7fl oz) unsweetened soya milk

Directions:

- Place all of the ingredients into a blender with enough water to cover them and process until smooth.

Nutrition:

- Calories: 150

- Fat: 9 g

- Sodium: 30 mg

- Carbohydrates: 17 g

- Protein: 3 g

- Fiber: 2 g

- Sugar: 14 g

Mushroom & Red Onion Buckwheat Pancakes

Preparation time: 5 minutes

Cooking time: 10 minutes

Servings: 2

Ingredients:

For the pancakes:

- 125g (4oz) buckwheat flour

- 1 egg

- 150mls (5fl oz) semi-skimmed milk

- 150mls (5fl oz) water

- 1 teaspoon olive oil for frying

For the filling:

- 1 red onion, chopped

- 75g (3½ oz) mushrooms, sliced

- 50g (2oz) spinach leaves

- 1 tablespoon fresh parsley, chopped

- 1 teaspoon olive oil

- 50g (2oz) rocket (arugula) leaves

Directions:

- Sift the flour into a bowl and mix in an egg.

- Pour in the milk and water and mix to a smooth batter. Set aside.

- Heat a teaspoon of olive oil in a pan. Add the onion and mushrooms and cook for 5 minutes.

- Add the spinach and allow it to wilt. Set aside and keep it warm. Heat a teaspoon of oil in a frying pan and pour in half of the batter.

- Cook for 2 minutes on each side until golden.

- Spoon the spinach and mushroom mixture onto the pancake and add the parsley.

- Fold it over and serve onto a scattering of rocket (arugula) leaves. Repeat for the remaining mixture.

Nutrition:

- Calories: 109

- Fat: 5 g

- Sodium: 61 mg

- Potassium: 339 mg

- Carbohydrates: 34 g

- Protein: 6 g

Cream of Broccoli & Kale Soup

Preparation time: 10 minutes

Cooking time: 30 minutes

Servings: 4

Ingredients:

- 250g (9oz) broccoli

- 250g (9oz) kale

- 1 potato, peeled and chopped

- 1 red onion, chopped

- 600mls (1 pint) vegetable stock

- 300mls (½ pint) milk

- 1 tablespoon olive oil

- Sea salt

- Freshly ground black pepper

Directions:

- Heat the olive oil in a saucepan, add the onion and cook for 5 minutes.

- Add in the potato, kale and broccoli and cook for 5 minutes.

- Pour in the stock (broth) and milk and simmer for 20 minutes.

- Using a food processor or hand blender, process the soup until smooth and creamy.

- Season it with salt and pepper.

Nutrition:

- Calories: 123

- Total Fat: 7 g

- Cholesterol: 16 mg

- Sodium: 528 mg

- Potassium: 667 mg

- Total Carbohydrates: 13.4 g

- Protein: 5 g

French Onion Soup

Preparation time: 10 minutes

Cooking time: 55 minutes

Servings: 4

Ingredients:

- 750g (1¾ lbs) red onions, thinly sliced

- 50g (2oz) Cheddar cheese, grated (shredded)

- 12g (½ oz) butter

- 2 teaspoons flour

- 2 slices Wholemeal bread

- 900mls (1½ pints) beef stock (broth)

- 1 tablespoon olive oil

Directions:

- Heat the butter and oil in a large pan. Add the onions and gently cook on a low heat for 25 minutes, stirring occasionally.

- Add in the flour and stir well. Pour in the stock (broth) and keep stirring.

- Bring to the boil, reduce the heat and simmer for 30 minutes.

- Cut the slices of bread into triangles, sprinkle with cheese and place them under a hot grill (broiler) until the cheese has melted.

- Serve the soup into bowls and add 2 triangles of cheesy toast on top. Enjoy.

Nutrition:

- Calories: 290

- Total Fat: 9 g

- Total Carbohydrates: 33 g

- Protein: 17 g

Cheesy Buckwheat Cakes

Preparation time: 4 minutes

Cooking time: 4 minutes

Servings: 2

Ingredients:

- 100g (3½oz) buckwheat, cooked and cooled

- 1 large egg

- 25g (1oz) cheddar cheese, grated (shredded)

- 25g (1oz) Wholemeal breadcrumbs

- 2 shallots, chopped

- 2 tablespoons fresh parsley, chopped

- 1 tablespoon olive oil

Directions:

- Crack the egg into a bowl, whisk it then set aside. In a separate bowl combine all the buckwheat, cheese, shallots and parsley and mix well.

- Pour in the beaten egg to the buckwheat mixture and stir well.

- Shape the mixture into patties. Scatter the breadcrumbs on a plate and roll the patties in them. Heat the olive oil in a large frying pan and gently place the cakes in the oil.

- Cook for 3-4 minutes on either side until slightly golden.

Nutrition:

- Calories: 240

- Total Fat: 4 g

- Sodium: 380 mg

- Total Carbohydrates: 40 g

- Protein: 11 g

Lentil Soup

Preparation time: 5 minutes

Cooking time: 55 minutes

Servings: 4

Ingredients:

- 175g (6oz) red lentils

- 1 red onion, chopped

- 1 clove of garlic, chopped

- 2 sticks of celery, chopped

- 2 carrots, chopped

- ½ bird eye chili

- 1 teaspoon ground cumin

- 1 teaspoon ground turmeric

- 1 teaspoon ground coriander (cilantro)

- 1200mls (2 pints) vegetable stock (broth)

- 2 tablespoons olive oil

- Sea salt

- Freshly ground black pepper

Directions:

- Heat the oil in a saucepan and add the onion and cook for 5 minutes.

- Add in the carrots, lentils, celery, chili, coriander (cilantro), cumin, turmeric and garlic and cook for 5 minutes.

- Pour in the stock (broth), bring it to the boil, reduce the heat and simmer for 45 minutes.

- Using a hand blender or food processor, puree the soup until smooth.

- Season it with salt and pepper. Serve.

Nutrition:

- Calories: 194

- Total Fat: 1 g

- Sodium: 231 mg

- Total Carbohydrates: 34 g

- Protein: 13

- Fiber: 2 g

Apple Pancakes

Preparation time: 15 minutes

Cooking time: 24 minutes

Servings: 6

Ingredients:

- ½ cup buckwheat flour

- 2 tablespoons coconut sugar

- 1 teaspoon baking powder

- ½ teaspoon ground cinnamon

- 1/3 cup unsweetened almond milk

- 1 egg, beaten lightly

- 2 granny smith apples, peeled, cored, and grated

Directions:

- In a bowl, place the flour, coconut sugar, and cinnamon, and mix well.

- In another bowl, place the almond milk and egg and beat until well combined.

- Now, place the flour mixture and mix until well combined.

- Fold in the grated apples.

- Heat a lightly greased non-stick wok over medium-high heat.

- Add desired amount of mixture and with a spoon, spread into an even layer.

- Cook for 1–2 minutes on each side.

- Repeat with the remaining mixture.

- Serve warm with the drizzling of honey.

Nutrition:

- Calories 93

- Total Fat 2.1 g

- Saturated Fat 1 g

- Cholesterol 27 mg

- Sodium 23 mg

- Total Carbohydrates 22 g

- Fiber 3 g

- Sugar 12.1 g

- Protein 2.5 g

Matcha Pancakes

Preparation time: 15 minutes

Cooking time: 24 minutes

Servings: 6

Ingredients:

- 2 tablespoons flax meal

- 5 tablespoons warm water

- 1 cup spelt flour

- 1 cup buckwheat flour

- 1 tablespoon matcha powder

- 1 tablespoon baking powder

- Pinch of salt

- ¾ cup unsweetened almond milk

- 1 tablespoon olive oil

- 1 teaspoon vanilla extract

- 1/3 cup raw honey

Directions:

- In a bowl, add the flax meal and warm water and mix well. Set aside for about 5 minutes.

- In another bowl, place the flours, matcha powder, baking powder, and salt, and mix well.

- In the bowl of flax meal mixture, place the almond milk, oil, and vanilla extract, and beat until well combined.

- Now, place the flour mixture and mix until a smooth textured mixture is formed.

- Heat a lightly greased non-stick wok over medium-high heat.

- Add desired amount of mixture and with a spoon, spread into an even layer.

- Cook for about 2–3 minutes.

- Carefully, flip the side and cook for about 1 minute.

- Repeat with the remaining mixture.

- Serve warm with the drizzling of honey.

Nutrition:

- Calories 232

- Total Fat 4.6 g

- Saturated Fat 0.6 g

- Cholesterol 0 mg

- Sodium 56 mg

- Total Carbohydrates 46.3 g

- Fiber 5.3 g

- Sugar 16.2 g

- Protein 6 g

Chocolate Muffins

Preparation time: 15 minutes

Cooking time: 20 minutes

Servings: 6

Ingredients:

- ½ cup buckwheat flour

- ½ cup almond flour

- 4 tablespoons arrowroot powder

- 4 tablespoons cacao powder

- 1 teaspoon baking powder

- ½ teaspoon bicarbonate soda

- ½ cup boiled water

- 1/3 cup maple syrup

- 1/3 cup coconut oil, melted

- 1 tablespoon apple cider vinegar

- ½ cup unsweetened dark chocolate chips

Directions:

- Preheat your oven to 350°F. Line 6 cups of a muffin tin with paper liners.

- In a bowl, place the flours, arrowroot powder, baking powder, and bicarbonate of soda, and mix well.

- In a separate bowl, place the boiled water, maple syrup, and coconut oil, and beat until well combined.

- Now, place the flour mixture and mix until just combined.

- Gently, fold in the chocolate chips.

- Transfer the mixture into prepared muffin cups evenly.

- Bake for about 20 minutes, or until a toothpick inserted in the center comes out clean.

- Remove the muffin tin from oven and place onto a wire rack to cool for about 10 minutes.

- Carefully invert the muffins onto the wire rack to cool completely before serving.

Nutrition:

- Calories 410

- Total Fat 28.6 g

- Saturated Fat 17.8 g

- Sodium 25 mg

- Total Carbohydrates 32.5 g

- Fiber 5.8 g

- Protein 4.6 g

Kale & Mushroom Frittata

Preparation time: 15 minutes

Cooking time: 30 minutes

Servings: 5

Ingredients:

- 8 eggs

- ½ cup unsweetened almond milk

- Salt and ground black pepper, to taste

- 1 tablespoon olive oil

- 1 onion, chopped

- 1 garlic clove, minced

- 1 cup fresh mushrooms, chopped

- 1½ cups fresh kale, tough ribs removed and chopped

Directions:

- Preheat oven to 350°F.

- In a large bowl, place the eggs, coconut milk, salt, and black pepper, and beat well. Set aside.

- In a large ovenproof wok, heat the oil over medium heat and sauté the onion and garlic for about 3–4 minutes.

- Add the squash, kale, bell pepper, salt, and black pepper, and cook for about 8–10 minutes.

- Stir in the mushrooms and cook for about 3–4 minutes.

- Add the kale and cook for about 5 minutes.

- Place the egg mixture on top evenly and cook for about 4 minutes, without stirring.

- Transfer the wok in the oven and bake for about 12–15 minutes or until desired doneness.

- Remove from the oven and place the frittata side for about 3–5 minutes before serving.

- Cut into desired sized wedges and serve.

Nutrition:

- Calories 151

- Total Fat 10.2 g

- Saturated Fat 2.6 g

- Cholesterol 262 mg

- Sodium 158 mg

- Total Carbohydrates 5.6 g

- Fiber 1 g

- Sugar 1.7 g

- Protein 10.3 g

Kale, Apple, and Cranberry Salad

Preparation time: 10 minutes

Cooking time: 15 minutes

Servings: 4

Ingredients:

- 6 cups fresh baby kale

- 3 large apples, cored and sliced

- ¼ cup unsweetened dried cranberries

- ¼ cup almonds, sliced

- 2 tablespoons extra-virgin olive oil

- 1 tablespoon raw honey

- Salt and ground black pepper, to taste

Directions:

- In a salad bowl, place all the ingredients and toss to coat well.

- Serve immediately.

Nutrition:

- Calories 253

- Total Fat 10.3 g

- Saturated Fat 1.2 g

- Cholesterol 0 mg

- Sodium 84 mg

- Total Carbohydrates 40.7 g

- Fiber 6.6 g

- Sugar 22.7 g

- Protein 4.7 g

Sirt Diet Recipes Cookbook

by

Lara Middleton

111

Additionally, the information in the following pages is intended only for informational purposes and should thus be thought of as universal. As befitting its nature, it is presented without assurance regarding its prolonged validity or interim quality. Trademarks that are mentioned are done without written consent and can in no way be considered an endorsement from the trademark holder.

Table of Contents

115

Breakfast Recipes

Kale Omelet

Preparation time: 5 minutes

Cooking time: 5 minutes

Serving: 1

Ingredients:

3 Eggs

1 small glove Garlic

2 handfuls Kale

Goat cheese or any cheese of your choice

¼ cup sliced onion

2 teaspoons extra virgin olive oil

Directions:

Mince the garlic, and finely shred the kale.

Break the eggs into a bowl, add a pinch of salt. Beat until well combined.

Place a pan to heat over medium heat. Add one teaspoon of olive oil, add the onion and kale, cook for approx. Five minutes, or until the onion has softened and the kale is wilted. Add the garlic and cook for another two minutes.

Add one teaspoon of olive oil into the egg mixture, mix and add into the pan. Use your spatula to move the cooked egg toward the center and move the pan so that the uncooked egg mixture goes towards the edges.

Add the cheese into the pan just before the egg is fully cooked, then leave for a minute.

Nutrition:

Calorie: 339

Carbohydrates: 30 g

Fat: 11 g

Protein: 30 g

Sirtfood Omelet

Preparation time: 5 minutes

Cooking time: 10 minutes

Serving: 1

Ingredients:

3 Medium eggs

2 ounces Sliced streaky bacon

1 ¼ ounces Red endive

1 teaspoon Turmeric

2 tablespoons Parsley (finely chopped)

1 teaspoon extra virgin olive oil - 1 teaspoon

Directions:

Place a nonstick fry pan to heat over medium-high heat. Add the bacon strips into the pan and cook until crispy. Do not add any oil as the bacon has enough fat to cook itself.

Put off the heat and place the bacon on a paper towel to drain any excess fat. Use a kitchen paper to wipe the pan clean.

Break the eggs into a bowl. Add the turmeric, parsley, and endive. Stir thoroughly. Cut the cooked bacon into cubes, add them into the bowl of the egg mixture and stir together.

Heat the olive oil in the frying pan until hot but not smoking. Then add the egg mixture and use a spatula to move it around the pan until the omelet is on an even level.

Reduce the heat and allow the omelet to firm up.

Use the spatula around the edges of the pan and roll up the omelet, or fold it in half.

Serve immediately.

Nutrition:

Calories: 154

Total Fat: 12 g

Cholesterol: 313 mg

Sodium: 155 mg

Potassium: 117 mg

Total Carbohydrates: 0.6 g

Protein: 11 g

Turmeric Scrambled Eggs

Preparation time: 10 min

Cooking time: 10 min

Servings: 3

Ingredients:

1 tablespoon Butter

1 handful large spinach

6 Large eggs

Salt & pepper to taste

2 teaspoons Turmeric powder

1 (chopped) large tomato

1 teaspoon Coconut oil

Directions:

Break the eggs into a medium bowl, whisk and add the pepper, salt, and turmeric. Mix together and set aside.

Heat the coconut oil in a small fry pan, add the chopped tomato and cook for about 2 to 3 minutes, until soft.

Add the spinach into the pan and cook for another two minutes. Set aside.

Add the butter into a small nonstick saucepan to melt under medium-low heat, and then add the egg mixture. Use your spatula to push the eggs from side to side across the pan.

Add the tomato and spinach to the pan when the eggs are almost done.

Once the egg is cooked, serve immediately.

Nutrition:

Calories: 208

Total Fat: 19 g

Total Carbohydrates: 31 g

Protein: 25 g

Sugar: 2 g

Fiber: 2 g

Salt: 1.4 g

Parsley Smoothie

Preparation time: 2 minutes

Cooking time: 2 minutes

Servings: 2

Ingredients:

1 cup Flat-leaf parsley

Juice of two lemons

1 (core removed) Apple

1 Avocado

1 cup Chopped kale

1 knob Peeled fresh ginger

1 tablespoon Honey

2 cups cold water

125

Directions:

Add all the ingredients except the avocado into your blender.

Blend on high until smooth, then add the avocado, then set your blender to slow speed and blend until creamy.

Add a little more iced water if the smoothie is too thick.

Nutrition:

Calories: 75

Total Fat: 1 g

Total Carbohydrates: 20 g

Protein: 1 g

Fiber: 2 g

Sodium: 26 mg

Matcha Overnight Oats

Preparation time: 5 minutes

Cooking time: 5 minutes

Servings: 2

Ingredients:

For the Oats

2 teaspoon Chia seeds

3 oz Rolled oats

1 teaspoon Matcha powder

1 teaspoon Honey

1 ½ cups Almond milk

2 pinches Ground cinnamon

For the Topping

1 Apple (peeled, cored and chopped)

A handful of mixed nuts

1 teaspoon Pumpkin seeds

Directions:

Get your oats ready a night before. Place the chia seeds and the oats in a container or bowl.

In a different jug or bowl, add the matcha powder and one tablespoon of almond milk and whisk with a hand-held mixer until you get a smooth paste, then add the rest of the milk and mix thoroughly.

Pour the milk mixture over the oats, add the honey and cinnamon, and then stir well. Cover the bowl with a lid and place in the fridge overnight.

When you want to eat, transfer the oats to two serving bowls, then top with the nuts, pumpkin seeds, and chopped apple.

Nutrition:

Calories: 300

Total Fat: 14 g

Total Carbohydrates: 37 g

Protein: 10 g

Yogurt with Mixed Berries, Dark Chocolate, and Chopped Walnuts

Preparation time: 2 minutes

Cooking time: 3 minutes

Serving: 1

Ingredients:

2 teaspoons Grated dark chocolate (85% cocoa solids)

1 cup Greek yogurt

1 cup Mixed berries

¼ cup (chopped) Walnuts

Directions:

129

Add your preferred berries into a serving bowl. Pour the yogurt on top.

Sprinkle with chocolate and walnuts.

Nutrition:

Calories: 70

Total Fat: 0 g

Cholesterol: 5 mg

Sodium: 80 mg

Potassium: 210 mg

Total Carbohydrates: 12 g

Sugars: 8 g

Protein: 5 g

Dark Chocolate Protein Truffles

Preparation time: 10 minutes

Cooking time: 15 minutes

Servings: 8

Ingredients:

¼ cup Coconut oil

¼ cup Vanilla whey protein powder

¼ cup (chopped) Medjool dates

¼ cup Almond milk

2 tablespoon Honey

⅛ Cup Steel-cut oats

1 tablespoon Coconut flour

2 Dark chocolate bars, minimum 85% cacao

Directions:

131

Mix the protein powder, honey, almond milk, dates, coconut flour, and oats in a bowl, then mold the mixture into eight balls.

Melt the coconut oil and chocolate over medium heat in a pot. Turn off the heat once melted and allow the chocolate to cool for about five to ten minutes. Dip each of the balls into the melted chocolate until well covered.

Place the balls in the freezer to harden.

Nutrition:

Calories: 65

Total Fat: 5 g

Total Carbohydrates: 2 g

Protein: 3 g

Homemade Kale Chips

Preparation time: 10 minutes

Cooking time: 14 minutes

Servings: 2 to 4

Ingredient:

5 ounces Kale (stalks taken off, washed and dried)

½ teaspoon Chili flakes

1 teaspoon Dried garlic granules

½ teaspoon Salt

1 tablespoon Nutritional yeast flakes

1 tablespoon extra-virgin olive oil

Directions:

Heat your oven to 300 degrees F.

Wash the kale clean and dry the leaves very well. Remove the woody stalks and break into bite-size pieces.

Place the kale into a bowl; sprinkle the remaining ingredients plus the olive oil. Use your fingers to massage the ingredients into the kale until well coated.

Place the coated kale into two baking trays, while ensuring that the leaves do not overlap.

Cook for approx. seven minutes, then rotate the tray and cook for another 7 minutes.

Allow to cool a little before you serve.

Nutrition:

Calories: 96.1

Total Fat: 7.3 g

Cholesterol: 0 mg

Sodium: 611.3 mg

Potassium: 296.5 mg

Total Carbohydrates: 7.3 g

Protein: 2.5 g

Refreshing Watermelon Juice

Preparation time: 2 minutes

Cooking time: 2 minutes

Serving: 1

Ingredients:

20g Young kale leaves (stalks removed)

½ Cucumber (peeled, seeds removed and roughly chopped)

250g Watermelon chunks

250g Mint leaves

Directions:

Add all the ingredients into your blender or juicer. Blend and enjoy.

135

Nutrition:

Calories: 76

Total Fat: 0 g

Total Carbohydrates: 17 g

Protein: 1 g

Matcha Granola with Berries

Preparation time: 10 minutes

Cooking time: 15 minutes

Servings: 4

Ingredients:

1 cup Rolled oats

2 tablespoon Coconut oil

½ cup (chopped) mixed nuts

1 tablespoon Pumpkin seeds

1 tablespoon Matcha powder

1 cup (halved or quartered) Strawberries

1 tablespoon Sesame seeds

½ teaspoon Ground cinnamon

3 tablespoons Runny honey

2/3 cup Blueberries

1 ¾ cups Greek yogurt

Directions:

Heat your oven to 325 degrees F. place parchment paper on a baking tray.

Heat the coconut oil under low heat until it melts. Put off the heat and stir in the seeds, nuts, and oats. Add the cinnamon, matcha powder, and honey, then mix thoroughly.

Evenly spread the granola mixture over the lined baking tray and place in the oven to bake for about fifteen minutes, until crisp and toasted – turn it 2 to 3 times.

Remove from the oven to cool, then store in an airtight container.

To serve, layer the yogurt in the serving dishes, then add the berries and granola.

Nutrition:

Calories: 490

Total Fat: 25 g

Sodium: 305 mg

Potassium: 507 mg

Total Carbohydrates: 59 g

Fiber: 9 g

Sugar: 24 g

Coffee and Cashew Smoothie

Preparation time: 2 minutes

Cooking time: 5 minutes

Serving: 1

Ingredients:

1 teaspoon Cashew butter

½ glass Chilled cashew

1 teaspoon Tahini

1 (pitted and chopped) Medjool date

1 shot Espresso coffee

½ teaspoon Ground cinnamon

Tiny pinch of salt

Directions:

Add all the ingredients into a high-speed blender. Blend until creamy and smooth.

Nutrition:

Calories: 125

Total Fat: 4 g

Sodium: 32 mg

Fiber: 3 g

Total Carbohydrates: 22 g

Protein: 3 g

Buckwheat Pita Bread Sirtfood

Preparation time: 5 minutes

Cooking time: 20 minutes

Servings: 6

Ingredients:

1 x 8 gram Packet dried yeast

375ml lukewarm water

3 tablespoon extra-virgin olive oil

500 grams Buckwheat flour

1 teaspoon Sea salt

Polenta for dusting

Directions:

142

Add the yeast in the lukewarm water, mix and set aside for about 10 to 15 minutes to activate.

Mix the buckwheat flour, olive oil, salt, and yeast mixture. Work slowly to make dough. Cover and place in a warm spot for approx. one hour – this is to get the dough to rise.

Divide the dough into six parts. Shape one of the pieces into a flat disc and place between two sheets of a baking paper. Gently roll out the dough into a round pita shape that is approximately ¼-inch thick. Use a fork to pierce the dough a few times, and then dust lightly with polenta.

Heat up your cast iron pan and brush the pan with olive oil. Cook the pita for about 5 minutes on one side, until puffy, and then turn to the other side and repeat.

Fill the pita with your preferred veggies and meat, and then serve immediately.

Nutrition:

Calories: 205

Total Fat: 7 g

Total Carbohydrates: 30 g

Protein: 6 g

No-Bake Apple Crisp

Preparation time: 5 minutes

Cooking time: 5 minutes

Servings: 8

Ingredients:

8 Apples (peeled, cored and chopped)

2 teaspoons Cinnamon (divided)

1 cup Raisins (soaked and drained)

2 tablespoons Lemon juice

1 cup Medjool dates

2 cups Walnuts

⅛ Teaspoon Sea salt

¼ teaspoon Nutmeg

Directions:

Add one teaspoon of cinnamon, the raisins, two apples, and the nutmeg into your food processor.

Toss the remaining chopped apples and the lemon juice in a big bowl.

Pour the apple puree over the apples in the bowl and mix well.

Transfer the mixture into a medium-sized baking dish and keep aside.

Add the remaining cinnamon, dates, sea salt, and walnuts into your food processor. Pulse until coarsely grounded. Do not over mix.

Sprinkle the mixture over the apples and use your hands to press down lightly.

Allow to sit for a few hours for the flavor to marinate or serve immediately.

Nutrition:

Calories: 164.2

Total Fat: 6.2 g

Sodium: 59.6 mg

Potassium: 121.0 mg

Total Carbohydrates: 28.3 g

Protein: 2.3 g

Matcha Latte

Preparation time: 2 minutes

Cooking time: 3 minutes

Serving: 1

Ingredients:

1 mug unsweetened rice milk

½ teaspoon Date syrup (optional)

1 teaspoon Matcha powder

Directions:

Heat the matcha and milk in a pan and froth it until it gets hot, stir in your preferred sweetener.

Pour into your cup and Enjoy!

Nutrition:

Calories: 85

Total Fat: 5 g

Total Carbohydrates: 8 g

Fiber: 2 g

Sugar: 6 g

Protein: 2 g

Lunch Recipes

Rocket salad with Tuna

Preparation time: 10 minutes

Cooking time: 15 minutes

Servings: 4

Ingredients:

4 slices rustic bread, torn into pieces

4 large tomatoes

2 Tbsp. olive oil

400g tin cannellini beans, drained and rinsed

¼ cup Kalamata olives

2 cups shredded rocket

149

¼ red onion, sliced finely

85g tin tuna

Dressing

2 tbsp. olive oil

½ tsp. Dijon mustard

1 tbsp. lemon juice

Directions:

Start with setting the oven at 180C. Place the bread slices in braking tray, put olive oil on slices and bake for 10-15 minutes.

To prepare the dressing mix lemon juice, mustard and oil in a jar.

Bring a bowl; add baked bread, onions, beans, tuna, tomatoes and rocket.

Put the dressing over salad and enjoy.

Nutrition:

Calories: 404

Total Fat: 15 g

Total Carbohydrates: 45 g

Protein: 17 g

Sirt Super Salad

Preparation time: 10 minutes

Cooking time: 10 minutes

Serving: 1

Ingredients:

1 3⁄4 ounces (50g) arugula

3 1⁄2 ounces (100g) smoked salmon slices

1 3⁄4 ounces (50g) endive leaves

1⁄2 cup (50g) celery including leaves, sliced

1⁄8 cups (15g) walnuts, chopped

1⁄2 cup (80g) avocado, peeled, stoned, and sliced

1⁄8 cup (20g) red onion, sliced

1 tablespoon extra-virgin olive oil

1 tablespoon capers

1 large Medjool date, pitted and chopped

1/4 cup (10g) parsley, chopped

¼ Juice of lemon

Directions:

Bring a bowl, place large leaves of salad, add all the ingredients one by one in the bowl and stir through the bowl and enjoy.

Nutrition:

Calories: 17

Total Fat: 0.3 g

Sodium: 8 mg

Total Carbohydrates: 3.3 g

Protein: 1.2 g

Strawberry Buckwheat Tabbouleh

Preparation time: 10 minutes

Cooking time: 10 minutes

Serving: 1

Ingredients:

1/3 cup (50g) buckwheat

1/2 cup (80g) avocado

1 tablespoon ground turmeric

1/8 cup (20g) red onion

3/8 cup (65g) tomato

1 tablespoon capers

1/8 cup (25g) Medjool dates, pitted

2/3 cup (100g) strawberries, hulled

3/4 cup (30g) parsley

1 tablespoon extra-virgin olive oil

1 ounce (30g) arugula

½ Juice of lemon

Directions:

Start with cooking the buckwheat by mixing the turmeric according to the instructions of package. Drain and let it cool.

Now, start chopping the tomatoes, capers, onions, avocados, dates and parsley. Mix all of them with already cooked buckwheat.

After that, take the strawberries, slice them and add them in salad. Garnish the salad on the arugula bed.

Nutrition:

Calories: 69

Total Fat: 5.7 g

Cholesterol: 0 mg

Total Carbohydrates: 3.8 g

Fiber: 1.2 g

Fragrant Asian Hotpot Sirtfood

Preparation time: 10 minutes

Cooking time: 15 minutes

Servings: 2

Ingredients:

1 tsp. tomato purée

1 star anise, crushed (or 1/4 tsp. ground anise)

Small handful (10g) parsley, stalks finely chopped

Small handful (10g) coriander, stalks finely chopped

Juice of 1/2 lime

1/2 carrot, peeled and cut into matchsticks

500ml chicken stock, fresh or made with 1 cube

50g beansprouts

100g firm tofu, chopped

50g broccoli, cut into small florets

155

100g raw tiger prawns

50g cooked water chestnuts, drained

50g rice noodles, cooked according to packet instructions

1 tbsp. good-quality miso paste

20g sushi ginger, chopped

Directions:

Take a pan and put the parsley stalks, lime juice, tomato purée, coriander stalks, star anise, and chicken stock, let them simmer for 10-12 minutes.

Now add the broccoli, tofu, carrot, water, chestnuts, and prawns, gently mix them and let them cook completely.

Turn off the heat and add in the miso paste and sushi ginger.

Garnish with coriander and parsley leaves and enjoy.

Nutrition:

Calories: 262

Total Fat: 6 g

Total Carbohydrates: 21 g

Protein: 24 g

Coronation Chicken Salad Sirtfood

Preparation time: 5 minutes

Cooking time: 5 minutes

Serving: 1

Ingredients:

75 g Natural yoghurt

1 tsp. Coriander, chopped

Juice of 1/4 of a lemon

1/2 tsp. Mild curry powder

1 tsp. Ground turmeric

6 Walnut halves, finely chopped

100 g Cooked chicken breast, cut into bite-sized pieces

20 g Red onion, diced

1 Bird's eye chili

1 Medjool date, finely chopped

40 g Rocket, to serve

Directions:

Take a bowl, gather the ingredients and mix them in bowl, and serve the salad on the rocket bedding.

Nutrition:

Calories: 111

Total Fat: 1 g

Total Carbohydrates: 8 g

Protein: 18 g

Buckwheat Pasta Salad

Preparation time: 5 minutes

Cooking time: 10 minutes

Serving: 1

Ingredients:

50g cooked buckwheat pasta

Small handful of basil leaves

Large handful of rockets

1/2 avocado, diced

1 tbsp. extra virgin olive oil

20g pine nuts

8 cherry tomatoes, halved

10 olives

159

Directions:

Take a bowl or a plate, add in all the ingredients, now scatter the pine nuts all over the ingredients and serve.

Nutrition:

Calories: 155

Total Fat: 1 g

Sodium: 252 mg

Total Carbohydrates: 33 g

Fiber: 4.5 g

Sugar: 1.5 g

Protein: 5.7 g

Salmon Sirt Super Salad

Preparation time: 10 minutes

Cooking time: 10 minutes

Serving: 1

Ingredients:

50g chicory leaves

80g avocado, peeled, stoned and sliced

50g rocket

40g celery, sliced

15g walnuts, chopped

100g smoked salmon slices

20g red onion, sliced

1 large Medjool date, pitted and chopped

1 tbsp. capers

Juice ¼ lemons

10g parsley, chopped

1 tbsp. extra-virgin olive oil

10g lovage or celery leaves, chopped

Directions:

Take a large bowl or plate. Put the large salad leave sin the plate. Add in all the ingredients and stir them well, now enjoy and serve.

Nutrition:

Calories: 17

Total Fat: 0.3 g

Sodium: 8 mg

Total Carbohydrates: 3.3 g

Protein: 1.2 g

Sesame Cucumber Salad

Preparation time: 10 minutes

Cooking time: 15 minutes

Servings: 3

Ingredients:

1 lb. Persian cucumbers

2 tbsp. sesame oil

1 tbsp. sesame seeds

1/2 tbsp. lemon juice

Kosher salt

Honey

1/3 c. cilantro, roughly chopped

163

1 tbsp. low-sodium soy sauce

1 tsp. grated peeled fresh ginger

Chili oil, for serving

Directions:

Take cucumbers and halve each of them lengthwise and, bash it slightly to crush, and then cut each half into 4 to 6 chunks. Transfer those cucumber chunks into a bowl and add 2 tsp. salt. Keep it aside 10 minutes.

In the meantime, add in together, honey, sesame seeds, oil, ginger, soy sauce and lemon juice together.

Rinse the cucumbers and shake off the water as much as possible by transferring them in colander.

Finely, add to the bowl with dressing and toss to combine, and then toss with cilantro. Serve drizzled with chili oil.

Nutrition:

Calories: 36.4

Total Fat: 1.3 g

Sodium: 3.4 mg

Potassium: 249.3 mg

Total Carbohydrates: 5.9 g

Protein: 1.5 g

Cowboy Caviar

Preparation time: 20 minutes

Cooking time: 2 hours

Servings: 5

Ingredients:

1/3 cup lime juice

1 cup fresh corn kernels, from about 2 ears

1 cup fresh corn kernels, from about 2 ears

1/2 cup fresh cilantro, chopped

1 15.5-oz cans black-eyed peas, rinsed

2 scallions, finely chopped

Salt and pepper

1 yellow pepper, finely chopped

1 large jalapeño, finely chopped

1/2 lb. Campari or plum tomatoes, cut into 1/4-inch pieces

1 tbsp. olive oil

Chips, for serving

Directions:

Start with taking a bowl; combine the garlic, salt, oil, lime juice and pepper.

Add in the jalapeno, peas, corn, tomatoes, yellow pepper and scallions.

Keep them in refrigerator for approximately 2 hours.

Garnish with cilantro and avocado and serve.

Nutrition:

Calories: 142.3

Total Fat: 4.9 g

Sodium: 85.4 mg

Potassium: 451.2 mg

Total Carbohydrates: 21.6 g

Protein: 5.7 g

Greek Salad

Preparation time: 10 minutes

Cooking time: 10 minutes

Servings: 4

Ingredients:

3 tbsp. red wine vinegar

2 tsp. confectioners' sugar

Salt and pepper

1 tsp. chopped fresh oregano

8 oz. cucumbers cut into 1/4-in.-thick rounds

1/2 very small red onion, thinly sliced

1/3 cup pitted Kalamata olives, halved

2 tbsp. capers, drained and roughly chopped

1 lb. mixed cherry, grape, and tomatoes (halved or cut into wedges)

2 tbsp. olive oil

Feta cheese, cut into small cubes, for serving

Directions:

Take a bowl; mix together vinegar, oil, sugar, and 1/4 teaspoon each salt and pepper. Stir in capers and oregano.

Now, arrange tomatoes and cucumbers on a platter and scatter onion and olives on top. Spoon dressing over salad and serve the salad with feta.

Nutrition:

Calories: 320

Total Fat: 22 g

Total Carbohydrates: 11 g

Protein: 19 g

Summer Squash Slaw with feta and Toasted Buckwheat

Preparation time: 5 minutes

Cooking time: 10 minutes

Servings: 4

Ingredients:

¼ cup buckwheat groats

2 scallions, thinly sliced

¼ cup coarsely chopped fresh mint

3 tablespoons olive oil

1 tablespoon fresh lemon juice

171

Salt, freshly ground pepper

1 teaspoon coarsely chopped fresh marjoram or oregano

1½ pounds yellow summer squash, julienned on a mandolin or with a knife

4 ounces feta, thinly sliced

Directions:

Start with toasting the buckwheat in a skillet over medium heat, approximately for 4-5 minutes. Put it to a plate; let it cool.

Add in mint, squash, oil, scallions, lemon juice, marjoram, and oil, sprinkle salt, pepper if you want.

In the end, put in buckwheat and feta and serve.

Nutrition:

Calories: 205

Total Fat: 16 g

Cholesterol: 25 mg

Sodium: 260 mg

Potassium: 19 mg

Total Carbohydrates: 9 g

Protein: 6 g

Buckwheat Noodles with Kimchi and Eggs

Preparation time: 10 minutes

Cooking time: 15 minutes

Servings: 4

Ingredients:

12 oz. Korean buckwheat noodles

1 12-oz. jar napa kimchi

1 tablespoon (or more) sugar

1 tablespoon toasted sesame oil

Salt

2 large eggs, hardboiled, quartered

4 scallions, thinly sliced

½ hot house cucumber, julienned

173

½ cup thinly sliced toasted laver or nori sheets

2 tablespoons toasted sesame seeds

2 tablespoons (or more) rice wine vinegar

Directions:

Take a large pot of water and boil it. Put noodles and cook, stirring occasionally, until cooked through, but still slightly bouncy, about 1½ minutes.

Drain and rinse under cold running water; put it aside.

Drain kimchi, reserving liquid; chop kimchi. Combine kimchi, kimchi liquid, vinegar, oil, and sugar in a large bowl and toss to combine.

Add the cooked noodles and toss to coat; season with salt and more vinegar or sugar.

Serve the dish with egg, cucumber, scallions, laver, sesame seeds, and 2 cups crushed ice.

Nutrition:

Calories: 511

Total Fat: 12 g

Total Carbohydrates: 89 g

Protein: 17 g

Vegan Buckwheat Risotto

Preparation time: 15 minutes

Cooking time: 15 minutes

Servings: 4

Ingredients:

250ml vegetable stock

1 big bunch of asparagus, chopped

2 cloves of garlic, minced

2 tablespoons macadamia, olive, or coconut oil, divided

1 small white onion, finely chopped

250g buckwheat, soaked overnight + drained and rinsed

1 small white onion, finely chopped

1 tablespoon dried Italian herbs

120g peas, fresh or thawed frozen

175

Large handful spinach, finely chopped

Salt + pepper

1 lemon, juiced and zested

Handful of parsley, oregano and basil, roughly chopped + more for topping

2 tablespoons nutritional yeast

Extra virgin olive oil, for drizzling

Directions:

Start with preparing veggie stock in a pan and boil them now dim the heat to simmer finely.

Take a large pan, heat 1 tbsp. of oil and fry your asparagus on light heat, until tender but still retains a bite -around 1 minute. Now, remove from the pan and put it aside.

Now, add the remaining oil along with the onion and garlic in the same pan and cook until soft, about 5 minutes. Put buckwheat, dried herbs, apple cider vinegar, and lemon juice to the pan and stir so that every ingredient is finely coated.

Put in veggie stock a little bit at a time, stirring occasionally, just like you would ordinary risotto.

Once the buckwheat is almost fully cooked, stir in your peas and spinach.

Cook more for few minutes then turn off the heat, stir in your herbs, lemon zest, nutritional yeast, salt and pepper. Taste and adjust seasoning, either putting in some more lemon juice or yeast for a cheesier flavour.

Use the asparagus, herbs and olive oil as toppings and serve.

Nutrition:

Calories: 24

Total Fat: 0.02 g

Total Carbohydrates: 0.24 g

Protein: 0.07 g

Miso marinated baked Cod with Stir fried Greens and Sesame seeds

Preparation time: 10 minutes

Cooking time: 15 minutes

Serving: 1

Ingredients:

20g miso

1 tbsp. extra virgin olive oil

1 tbsp. mirin

20g red onion, sliced

200g skinless cod fillet

1 garlic clove, finely chopped

40g celery, sliced

1 tsp. finely chopped fresh ginger

50g kale, roughly chopped

1 bird's eye chili, finely chopped

5g parsley, roughly chopped

60g green beans

1 tbsp. tamari

30g buckwheat

1 tsp. sesame seeds

1 tsp. ground turmeric

Directions:

Firstly, mix the miso, mirin and 1 teaspoon of the oil. Rub all over the cod and leave to marinate for 30 minutes. Now, preheat the oven to 220°C/gas 7.

Start baking the cod for almost 10 minutes.

Meantime heat a pan or wok with the remaining oil. Add the onion and stir-fry for a few minutes, then add the celery, garlic, chili, ginger, green beans and kale. Toss and fry until the kale is tender and cooked through.

Start cooking the buckwheat by following packet instructions with the turmeric for 3 minutes.

Add the sesame seeds, parsley and tamari to the stir-fry and enjoy with the greens and fish.

Nutrition:

Calories: 227

Total Fat: 3 g

Cholesterol: 60 mg

Sodium: 634 mg

Potassium: 30 mg

Total Carbohydrates: 15 g

Protein: 30 g

Dinner Recipes

Red Wine Marinated Grilled Tuna Steaks

Preparation time: 10 minutes

Cooking time: 30 minutes

Servings: 3

Ingredients:

4 (5 ounce) fresh tuna steaks, 1 inch thick

¼ cup soy sauce

½ cup dry red wine

¼ cup extra virgin olive oil

1 tablespoon fresh squeezed lime juice

1 clove garlic, minced

Directions:

182

Place tuna steaks in a shallow baking dish.

In a medium bowl, mix soy sauce, red wine, olive oil, lime juice, and garlic.

Pour the soy sauce mixture over the tuna steaks and turn to coat.

Cover, and refrigerate for at least one hour.

Preheat grill for high heat.

Lightly oil the grill grate and place tuna steaks on grill, discarding remaining marinade.

Grill for 3 to 6 minutes per side, or to desired firmness.

Nutrition:

Calories: 306

Fat: 8.9 g

Fiber: 11.1 g

Carbohydrates: 23.8 g

Protein: 14.5 g

Matcha Green Tea Salmon

Preparation time: 10 minutes

Cooking time: 20 minutes

Servings: 3

Ingredients:

4 (5 oz.) salmon fillets

2 tablespoons of extra virgin olive oil

2 tablespoons of fresh squeezed lemon juice

1 teaspoon of Matcha green tea powder

½ cup of wholegrain breadcrumbs

Salt and pepper to taste

Directions:

Preheat the oven to 350 degrees F.

184

While the oven is heating, add the olive oil, lemon juice, Matcha green tea powder, wholegrain breadcrumbs, salt and pepper to the large bowl and knead all the ingredients together using your hands.

Place the salmon fillets in the large bowl and cover them each with the breadcrumb mixture, pressing or patting into the fillet as needed. Place salmon fillets on a baking tray and bake them for 20 minutes.

Nutrition:

Calories: 207

Carbohydrates: 31 g

Protein: 5.1 g

Fat: 7 g

Tuscan Garlic Chicken

Preparation time: 10 minutes

Cooking time: 40 minutes

Servings: 3

Ingredients:

2 tablespoons extra virgin olive oil

¼ teaspoon dried parsley

¼ teaspoon dried oregano

¼ teaspoon dried lovage

1 teaspoon garlic powder

½ cup Parmesan cheese

1 cup arugula, chopped

½ cup sundried tomatoes

186

1/3 cup capers, drained

Directions:

Warm the olive oil in a large pan on medium heat. Add the chicken and cook for 3-5 minutes until brown all over.

When the chicken is no longer pink in the center, remove it from heat and set aside on a plate.

Add the chicken broth, heavy cream, garlic powder, parsley, oregano, lovage, and Parmesan cheese to the pan. Whisk on medium heat until it thickens.

Add the arugula, sundried tomatoes and capers, allowing them to simmer, until the arugula starts to wilt.

Then add the chicken back to the mixture in the pan to reheat for 1 minute before serving.

Nutrition:

Calories: 285

Carbs: 46.2 g

Protein: 8.5 g

Fat: 7.4 g

Baked Walnut Chicken Breast

Preparation time: 10 minutes

Cooking time: 50 minutes

Servings: 3

Ingredients:

¼ cup of walnuts, chopped

2 tbsp. extra virgin olive oil

2 boneless, skinless chicken breasts

Directions:

Preheat the oven to 350 degrees F.

188

Slice a deep groove into the middle of each chicken breast using a sharp knife and place the chopped walnuts in this groove, pouring the olive oil over top.

Put the chicken breasts on a baking tray and bake for 20 minutes.

Nutrition:

Calories: 202

Carbs: 21 g

Protein: 8 g

Fat: 10 g

Roast Duck with Apple Dressing

Preparation time: 10 minutes

Cooking time: 70 minutes

Servings: 3

Ingredients:

1 (4 pound) whole duck

Salt and pepper to taste

1 teaspoon poultry seasoning

2 tablespoon extra-virgin olive oil

3 tablespoons red onion, chopped

5 stalks celery, chopped

3 cups, chopped

3 cups cornbread crumbs

Directions:

190

Preheat oven to 350 degrees F.

Rinse the duck and pat dry. Rub with salt, pepper, and poultry seasoning, to taste.

Heat 1 tablespoon of the olive oil in a small skillet over medium heat. Sauté onion and celery until it tender.

In a medium bowl, combine with apple and cornbread crumbs with the onion-celery mixture.

Mix together to make stuffing, add little water to moisten if necessary. Fill the duck's cavity with the stuffing and sew shut with kitchen twine. Rub the outside of bird lightly with the remaining tablespoon of olive oil, and place in a shallow roasting pan or 9x13 inch baking dish.

Bake in preheated oven for 60 to 80 minutes, or until internal temperature reaches 180 degrees F.

Nutrition:

Calories: 282

Fat: 18.6 g

Fiber: 4 g

Carbohydrates: 9 g

Protein: 18 g

Shrimp Asparagus Alfredo

Preparation time: 10 minutes

Cooking time: 30 minutes

Servings: 3

Ingredients:

1 pound fettuccine noodles, cooked al dente

1 pound shrimp, peeled and deveined

6 tablespoons unsalted butter, divided

6 garlic slice

1 cup heavy cream

1 cup half

1/2 tsp. ground nutmeg

1/3 cup Parmesan cheese

192

1 cup blanched asparagus, cut into pieces

Parsley

Salt & pepper

Directions:

Season the shrimp with salt.

Melt 3 tbsps. of butter in a large skillet. Shrimp until cooked, then remove the shrimp.

Add the remaining butter to the Pan. Whisk in the cream and nutmeg. Season it with salt and pepper. Garnish with a sprinkle of chopped parsley.

Nutrition:

Calories: 52

Complete Fat 42 g

Immersed Fat 5.8 g

Cholesterol 32 mg

Sodium 25 mg

Potassium 65 mg

Starches 5 g

Chicken Ayam

Preparation time: 10 minutes

Cooking time: 40 minutes

Servings: 3

Ingredients:

1 sliced red chili

1 teaspoon of ginger

1 small red onion, sliced

1 teaspoon turmeric

1 teaspoon galangal

4 cloves of garlic

1 pinch black pepper

3 tips muscovado sugar

3 tsp. shrimp paste

1/3 cup coconut milk

Directions:

Season the chicken legs. Put on low heat on the grill for about 10 min on one side.

Bring all the ingredients together as finely as possible using a mortar and pestle or a blender.

Fry in some peanut oil. Put some paste on the chicken.

Cook the other side for about 5 minutes. Add some glue to the chicken.

Move to the hotter side of the grill, flip, baste and cook for three additional minutes on both sides. Grill the cake on both sides.

Nutrition:

Calories: 41 g

Fat: 2.3 g

Cholesterol: 35mg

Sodium: 75 mg

Potassium: 7g

Starches: 61 mcg

Calcium: 45 mg

Garbanzo Kale Curry

Preparation time: 10 minutes

Cooking Time: 30 minutes

Servings 8

Ingredients:

4 cups dry garbanzo beans

Curry Paste, but go low on the heat

1 cup sliced tomato

2 cups kale leaves

1/2 cup coconut milk

Directions:

196

Put ingredients in the slow cooker. Cover, & cook on low for 30 minutes.

Nutrition:

Calories: 282

Total Fat: 12.6g

Carbohydrates: 11.5g

Protein: 17.3g

Tomato Frittata

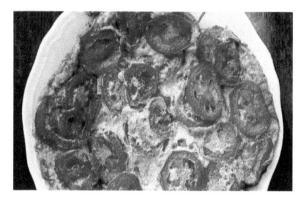

Preparation time: 15 minutes

Cooking time: 20 minutes

Servings: 2

Ingredients:

50g cheddar cheese, grated

75g kalamata olives, pitted and halved

8 cherry tomatoes, halved

4 large eggs

1 tbsp. fresh parsley, chopped

1 tbsp. fresh basil, chopped

1 tbsp. olive oil

Directions:

Whisk eggs together in a large mixing bowl. Toss in the parsley, basil, olives, tomatoes and cheese, stirring thoroughly.

In a small skillet, heat the olive oil over high heat. Pour in the frittata mixture and cook for 5-10 minutes, or set.

Remove the skillet from the hob and place under the grill for 5 minutes, or until firm and set. Divide into portions and serve immediately.

Nutrition:

Calories: 269

Protein: 9.23 g

Fat: 23.76 g

Carbohydrates: 5.49 g

Horseradish Flaked Salmon Fillet & Kale

Preparation time: 15 minutes

Cooking time: 30 minutes

Servings: 2

Ingredients:

200g skinless, boneless salmon fillet

50g green beans

75g kale

1 tbsp. extra virgin olive oil l

½ garlic clove, crushed

50g red onion, chopped

1 tbsp. fresh chives, chopped

1 tbsp. freshly chopped flat-leaf parsley

1 tbsp. low fat crème fraiche

1tbsp horseradish sauce

Juice of ¼ lemons

Directions:

Preheat the grill.

Sprinkle a salmon fillet with salt and pepper. Place under the grill for 10-15 minutes. Flake and set aside.

Using a steamer, cook the kale and green beans for 10 minutes.

In a skillet, warm the oil over a high heat. Add garlic and red onion and fry for 2-3 minutes. Toss in the kale and beans, and then cook for 1-2 minutes more.

Mix the chives, parsley, crème fraiche, horseradish, lemon juice and flaked salmon.

Serve the kale and beans topped with the dressed flaked salmon.

Nutrition:

Calories: 206 kcal

Protein: 26.7 g

Fat: 6 g

Carbohydrates: 11 g

Greek Sea Bass Mix

Preparation time: 10 minutes

Cooking time: 22 minutes

Servings: 2

Ingredients:

2 sea bass fillets, boneless

1 garlic clove, minced

5 cherry tomatoes, halved

1 tablespoon chopped parsley

2 shallots, chopped

Juice of ½ lemons

1 tablespoon olive oil

8 ounces baby spinach

Cooking spray

Directions:

Grease a baking dish with cooking oil then add the fish, tomatoes, parsley and garlic. Drizzle the lemon juice over the fish, cover the dish and place it in the oven at 350 degrees F. Bake for 15 minutes and then divide between plates. Heat up a pan with the olive oil over medium heat, add shallot, stir and cook for 1 minute. Add spinach, stir, cook for 5 minutes more, add to the plate with the fish and serve. Enjoy!

Nutrition:

Calories: 210

Fat: 3 g

Fiber: 6 g

Carbohydrates: 10 g

Protein: 24 g

Pomegranate Guacamole

Preparation time: 10 minutes

Cooking Time: 30 minutes

Servings 4

Ingredients:

Flesh of 2 ripe avocados

Seeds from 1 pomegranate

1 bird's-eye chili pepper, finely chopped

½ red onion, finely chopped

Juice of 1 lime

151 calories per serving

Directions:

Place the avocado, onion, chill and lime juice into a blender and process until smooth.

Stir in the pomegranate seeds.

Chill before serving. Serve as a dip for chop vegetables.

Nutrition:

Calories: 127

Carbohydrates: 13 g

Protein: 7 g

Fat: 5 g

Cajun Steak and Veg Rice Jar Recipe

Preparation time: 10 minutes

Cooking time: 25 minutes

Servings: 3

Ingredients:

1 tablespoon vegetable oil

1 celery stick, finely chopped

3 large carrots, sliced into rounds

250g frozen chopped mixed peppers

4 spring onions, chopped, green and white parts split

500g 5 percent beef mince

2 teaspoon seasoning

1 teaspoon tomato purée

2 x 250g packs ready-cooked long-grain rice

Directions:

Heat the oil in a large, shallow skillet over moderate heat. Add the carrots, celery, peppers and frozen peppers. Cook for 10 minutes before the vegetable is beginning to soften.

Insert the mince, season liberally and cook for 10 minutes before mince is browned and start to get crispy.

Add the Cajun seasoning and tomato purée; stir fry to coat the mince. Place with the rice, combined with 4 tablespoons of plain water. Stir to completely combine until the rice is hot. Sprinkle on the rest of the spring onion before serving.

Nutrition:

Calories: 456

Fat: 12 g

Sugar: 13 g

Sodium: 1 g

Carbohydrates: 53 g

Protein: 32 g

Fiber: 8 g

Roast Duck Legs with Red Wine Sauce

Preparation time: 10 minutes

Cooking time: 1 hour

Servings: 3

Ingredients:

1 bunch fresh rosemary, chopped

4 large garlic cloves

4 duck legs

Salt to taste

1 teaspoon Chinese five-spice powder

1 ½ cups red wine

1 ½ tablespoons red currant jelly

Directions:

208

Preheat an oven to 375 degrees.

Spread the rosemary sprigs and whole garlic cloves into a 9x13-inch baking dish.

Place the duck legs on top of the rosemary, and sprinkle with salt and five-spice powder. Bake in the preheated oven for 1 hour.

Meanwhile, bring the wine to a boil in a small saucepan over medium-high heat. After the duck has cooked 1 hour, pour off and discard the fat that has accumulated in the baking dish. Pour the wine sauce over the duck legs and bake 15 minutes more until the duck is very tender and the sauce has thickened slightly.

Nutrition:

Calories: 282

Total Fat: 10.2 g

Carbohydrates: 8 g

Protein: 15 g

Snacks Recipes

Crunchy Potato Bites

Preparation time: 10 minutes

Cooking time: 20 minutes

Servings: 5

Ingredients:

1 potato, sliced

2 bacon slices, already cooked and crumbled

1 small avocado, pitted and cubed

1 tbsp. of extra virgin olive oil

Directions:

211

Spread potato slices on a lined baking sheet.

Toss around with the extra virgin olive oil.

Insert in the oven at 350 degrees F.

Bake for 20 minutes.

Arrange on a platter, top each slice with avocado and crumbled bacon and serve as a snack.

Nutrition:

Calories: 230

Total Fat: 14 g

Carbohydrates: 25 g

Protein: 2 g

Sprouts and Apples Snack Salad

Preparation time: 10 minutes

Cooking time: 10 minutes

Servings: 5

Ingredients:

1 pound Brussels sprouts, shredded

1 cup walnuts, chopped

1 apple, cored and cubed

1 red onion, chopped

For the salad dressing:

3 tablespoons red vinegar

1 tablespoon mustard

½ cup olive oil

213

1 garlic clove, minced

Black pepper to the taste

Directions:

In a salad bowl, mix sprouts with apple, onion and walnuts.

In another bowl, mix vinegar with mustard, oil, garlic, and pepper and whisk really well.

Add the dressing to your salad, toss well and serve as a snack.

Nutrition:

Calories: 46

Total Fat: 2 g

Total Carbohydrates: 6 g

Protein: 2.2 g

Moroccan Snack Salad

Preparation time: 10 minutes

Cooking time: 10 minutes

Servings: 5

Ingredients:

1 bunch radishes, sliced

3 cups leeks, chopped

1 and ½ cups olives, pitted and sliced

A pinch of turmeric powder

Black pepper to the taste

2 tablespoons olive oil

1 cup cilantro, chopped

Directions:

215

In a bowl, mix radishes with leeks, olives and cilantro.

Add black pepper, oil and turmeric, toss to coat and serve as a snack.

Nutrition:

Calories: 121

Total Fat: 12 g

Total Carbohydrates: 15 g

Protein: 27 g

Celery and Raisins Snack Salad

Preparation time: 10 minutes

Cooking time: 10 minutes

Servings: 3

Ingredients:

½ cup raisins

4 cups celery, sliced

¼ cup parsley, chopped

½ cup walnuts, chopped

Juice of ½ lemons

2 tablespoons olive oil

Salt and black pepper to the taste

Directions:

In a salad bowl, mix celery with raisins, walnuts, parsley, lemon juice, oil, and black pepper and toss.

Divide into small cups and serve as a snack.

Nutrition:

Calories: 267

Total Fat: 11 g

Cholesterol: 1.3 mg

Sodium: 59 mg

Total Carbohydrates: 42 g

Protein: 5 g

Spicy Pumpkin Seeds Bowl

Preparation time: 10 minutes

Cooking time: 20 minutes

Servings: 5

Ingredients:

½ tablespoon chili powder

½ teaspoon cayenne pepper

2 cups pumpkin seeds

2 teaspoons lime juice

Directions:

Spread pumpkin seeds on a lined baking sheet, add lime juice, cayenne and chili powder, and toss well.

Put it in the oven and roast at 275 degrees F for 20 minutes.

Divide into small bowls and serve as a snack.

Nutrition:

Calories: 144

Total Fat: 16 g

Sodium: 75 mg

Potassium: 269 mg

Total Carbohydrates: 5 g

Protein: 11 g

Apple and Pecan Bowls

Preparation time: 10 minutes

Cooking time: 10 minutes

Servings: 4

Ingredients:

4 big apples, cored, peeled and cubed

2 teaspoons lemon juice

¼ cup pecans, chopped

Directions:

In a bowl, mix apples with lemon juice, and pecans and toss.

Divide into small bowls and serve as a snack.

221

Nutrition:

Calories: 230

Total Fat: 17 g

Total Carbohydrates: 15 g

Cheesy Mushrooms

Preparation time: 10 minutes

Cooking time: 30 minutes

Servings: 5

Ingredients:

20 white mushroom caps

1 garlic clove, minced

3 tablespoons parsley, chopped

2 yellow onions, chopped

Black pepper to the taste

½ cup low-fat parmesan, grated

¼ cup low-fat mozzarella, grated

A drizzle of olive oil

2 tablespoons non-fat yogurt

Directions:

223

Heat up a pan with some oil over medium heat, add garlic and onion, stir, cook for 10 minutes and transfer to a bowl.

Add black pepper, garlic, parsley, mozzarella, parmesan and yogurt, stir well, stuff the mushroom caps with the mix.

Arrange them on a lined baking sheet and bake in the oven at 400 degrees F for 20 minutes.

Serve them as an appetizer.

Nutrition:

Calories: 100

Total Fat: 7 g

Cholesterol: 22.2 mg

Sodium: 202 mg

Potassium: 195 mg

Total Carbohydrates: 2.5 g

Protein: 6 g

Shrimp Muffins

Preparation time: 10 minutes

Cooking time: 45 minutes

Servings: 6

Ingredients:

1 spaghetti squash, peeled and halved

2 tablespoons avocado mayonnaise

1 cup low-fat mozzarella cheese, shredded

8 ounces shrimp, peeled, cooked and chopped

1 and ½ cups almond flour

1 teaspoon parsley, dried

1 garlic clove, minced

Black pepper to the taste

Cooking spray

Directions:

Arrange the squash on a lined baking sheet.

Insert in the oven at 375 degrees F and bake for 30 minutes.

Scrape squash flesh into a bowl and add pepper, parsley flakes, flour, shrimp, mayo, and mozzarella and stir well.

Divide this mix into a muffin tray greased with cooking spray.

Bake in the oven at 375 degrees F for 15 minutes.

Serve them cold as a snack.

Nutrition:

Calories: 321

Total Fat: 16 g

Cholesterol: 49 mg

Sodium: 393 mg

Total Carbohydrates: 35 g

Protein: 9 g

Mozzarella Cauliflower Bars

Preparation time: 10 minutes

Cooking time: 40 minutes

Servings: 12

Ingredients:

1 big cauliflower head, riced

½ cup low-fat mozzarella cheese, shredded

¼ cup egg whites

1 teaspoon Italian seasoning

Black pepper to the taste

Directions:

Spread the riced cauliflower on a lined baking sheet and cook in the oven at 375 degrees F for 20 minutes.

Transfer to a bowl, add black pepper, cheese, seasoning and egg whites, stir well, spread into a rectangle pan and press well on the bottom.

Introduce in the oven at 375 degrees F and bake for 20 minutes.

Let it cool and cut into 12 bars

Serve at room temperature as a snack.

Nutrition:

Total Fat: 5 g

Cholesterol: 33 mg

Sodium: 297 mg

Potassium: 172 mg

Total Carbohydrates: 3.8 g

Fiber: 1.4 g

Protein: 6 g

Cinnamon Apple Chips

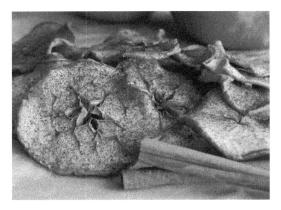

Preparation time: 10 minutes

Cooking time: 2 hours

Servings: 4

Ingredients:

Cooking spray

2 teaspoons cinnamon powder

2 apples, cored and thinly sliced

Directions:

Arrange apple slices on a lined baking sheet, spray them with cooking oil, and sprinkle cinnamon on it.

Put it in the oven and bake at 300 degrees F for 2 hours.

Divide into bowls and serve as a snack.

Nutrition:

Calories: 110

Total Carbohydrates: 27 g

Fiber: 4 g

Sugar: 21 g

Vegetable and Nuts Bread Loaf

Preparation time: 15 minutes

Cooking time: 1 hour and 10 minutes

Servings: 1

Ingredients:

1 loaf

175g (6oz) mushrooms, finely chopped

100g (3½ oz) haricot beans

100g (3½ oz) walnuts, finely chopped

100g (3½ oz) peanuts, finely chopped

1 carrot, finely chopped

3 sticks celery, finely chopped

1 bird's-eye chili, finely chopped

1 red onion, finely chopped

1 egg, beaten

231

2 cloves of garlic, chopped

2 tablespoons olive oil

2 teaspoons turmeric powder

2 tablespoons soy sauce

4 tablespoons fresh parsley, chopped

100mls (3½ oz) water

60mls (2fl oz) red wine

Directions:

Heat the oil in a pan and add the garlic, chili, carrot, celery, onion, mushrooms and turmeric.

Cook for 5 minutes.

Place the haricot beans in a bowl and stir in the nuts, vegetables, soy sauce, egg, parsley, red wine and water.

Grease and line a large loaf tin with greaseproof paper.

Spoon the mixture into the loaf tin, cover with foil and bake in the oven at 190C/375F for 60-90 minutes.

Let it stand for 10 minutes then turn onto a serving plate.

Nutrition:

Calories: 199

Total Fat: 12 g

Cholesterol: 132.8 mg

Sodium: 168 mg

Potassium: 368 mg

Total Carbohydrates: 16.3 g

Protein: 9 g

Almond Crackers

Preparation time: 15 minutes

Cooking time: 30 minutes

Servings: 40

Ingredients:

40 crackers

1 cup almond flour

¼ teaspoon baking soda

1/8 teaspoon black pepper

3 tablespoons sesame seeds

1 egg, beaten

Salt and pepper to taste

Directions:

Pre-heat your oven to 350 degrees F.

Line two baking sheets with parchment paper and keep them on the side.

Mix the dry ingredients in a large bowl and add egg, mix well and form dough.

Divide dough into two balls.

Roll out the dough between two pieces of parchment paper.

Cut into crackers and transfer them to prepared baking sheet.

Bake for 15-20 minutes.

Repeat until all the dough has been used up.

Leave crackers to cool and serve as needed as a snack or with one or more of the spreads as appetizers.

Nutrition:

Calories: 130

Total Fat: 2 g

Cholesterol:

Sodium: 115 mg

Total Carbohydrates: 24 g

Protein: 3 g

Sweet Bites

Preparation time: 10 minutes

Cooking time: 1 hour

Servings: 15

Ingredients:

120g walnuts

30g dark chocolate (85% cocoa)

250g dates

1 tablespoon pure cocoa powder

1 tablespoon turmeric

1 tablespoon of olive oil

Contents of a vanilla pod or some vanilla flavoring

Directions:

236

Coarsely crumble the chocolate and mix it with the walnuts in a food processor into a fine powder. Then add the other ingredients and stir until you have uniform dough.

If necessary, add 1 to 2 tablespoons of water.

Form 15 pieces from the mixture and refrigerate in an airtight tin for at least one hour.

The bites will remain in the refrigerator for a week.

Nutrition:

Calories: 210

Total Fat: 14 g

Cholesterol: 10 mg

Sodium: 230 mg

Carbohydrates: 22 g

Protein: 2 g

Cocoa Bars

Preparation time: 20 minutes

Cooking time: 2 hours

Servings: 12

Ingredients:

1 cup unsweetened cocoa chips

2 cups rolled oats

1 cup low-fat peanut butter

½ cup chia seeds

½ cup raisins

¼ cup coconut sugar

½ cup coconut milk

Directions:

238

Put 1 and ½ cups oats in your blender and pulse well

Transfer the shredded oats to a bowl, add the rest of the oats, cocoa chips, chia seeds, raisins, sugar, and milk and stir really well.

Spread the paste into a square pan, press well, and keep in the fridge for at least 2 hours

Slice into 12 bars and serve or conserve in the fridge.

Nutrition:

Calories: 260

Fat: 21 g

Sodium: 20 mg

Carbohydrates: 14 g

Protein: 4 g

Lightning Source UK Ltd.
Milton Keynes UK
UKHW020742030621
384855UK00001B/271